The Underground Sea

The Underground Sea

Miners and the Miners' Strike

Edited by Tom Overton
and Matthew Harle

John Berger

CANONGATE

This Canons edition published in 2025 by Canongate Books

First published in Great Britain in 2024
by Canongate Books Ltd, 14 High Street, Edinburgh EH1 1TE

canongate.co.uk

1

Copyright © John Berger and the Estate of John Berger,
1963, 1968, 1972, 1989
Introduction copyright © Tom Overton and Matthew Harle, 2024
Text and images from *Germinal* copyright
© BBC Open University, 1973

The editors acknowledge the support of the Open University
towards the publication of this work

The right of John Berger, Tom Overton and Matthew Harle to be
identified as the authors of this work has been asserted by them
in accordance with the Copyright, Designs and Patents Act 1988

No part of this book may be used or reproduced in any manner for the purpose of
training artificial intelligence technologies or systems. This work is reserved from
text and data mining (Article 4(3) Directive (EU) 2019/790).

British Library Cataloguing-in-Publication Data
A catalogue record for this book is available on
request from the British Library

ISBN 978 1 83726 038 6

Text design by Scott King and Tom Etherington

Printed and bound in Great Britain by CPI Group (UK) Ltd,
Croydon CR0 4YY

The manufacturer's authorised representative in the EU for product safety is
Authorised Rep Compliance Ltd, 71 Lower Baggot Street, Dublin D02 P593 Ireland
(arccompliance.com)

Contents

Introduction 1
Miners 15
Germinal 20
Before My Time 89
The Nature of Mass Demonstrations 113

Introduction
Tom Overton & Matthew Harle

In the poem 'Self-Portrait 1914–18', John Berger set out what he saw as the historical co-ordinates of his life:

> It seems now that I was so near to that war.
> I was born eight years after it ended
> When the General Strike had been defeated

His father Stanley had been an infantry captain in the trenches of the Western Front. In civilian life he helped found the modern science of industrial accounting, travelling widely to spread its methods. On one of these trips, he took the sixteen-year-old Berger down a coal mine for the first time. This must have been just before wartime coal shortages got to the point, in 1943, when one in ten conscripts began to be sent down as 'Bevin Boys'. It was widely considered a worse fate than being sent to the front line.

By then, Berger was reading George Orwell, whose *The Road to Wigan Pier* (1937) has a chapter trying to get a feel for the cramped realities of the work from the perspective of a six-foot-two ex-public schoolboy. Things had improved a little since the nineteenth century, Orwell thought, but it was still the archetypical manual labour: invisible, 'awful', and necessary for the comfortable life which went on above. War on or not, Orwell was sympathetic when 100,000 Welsh miners went out on strike in 1944 and won a better minimum wage.

That was the year Berger was called up to the army: a public schoolboy among working-class recruits. His work as a young painter had a note of Orwell's witnessing to it, clocking on at the same time as the slightly bemused workers in factories and railway sidings, painting alongside them, trying to earn their trust. There was also the example of one of his drawing teachers, Henry Moore, a miner's son who had produced drawings of miners at work during the war.

Meanwhile, Berger started writing about exhibitions, town planning, and even fiction, including that by Émile Zola, a writer Orwell had once tried to get work translating. The Rougon-Macquart series, twenty connected novels about the booming of Paris as the French Second Empire (1852–70) declined and fell, and based on scrupulous research put to imaginative use, was one model for how to think about the rebuilding of blitzed London as its colonial power ebbed away.

As Berger's career as a Marxist art critic developed, one of the painters he returned to was the Jewish Polish émigré Josef Herman, who had settled in 1944 in the Welsh village of Ystradgynlais: a couple of hours' drive away from where Berger himself lived in the Forest of Dean. In Berger's view at least, Herman's work showed the miner as 'a walking monument to human labour'. His work 'contained a new, positive message', and expressed 'the endurance of labour and the grandeur of the landscape with the slag tips leaning against sullen skies'. If there's a sense of class tourism to Orwell's work, one of the things which particularly impressed Berger about Herman was the way he had become part of his community: an artist working alongside workers in much the way he'd tried to in his own painting career. It seemed connected to the images themselves: 'figures in landscape that "belong", that seem to have grown like trees in soil which is theirs'.

For a while, Berger hoped this form of indigenous realist painting would triumph in England and help people 'know and claim their social rights'. It didn't, and he moved away to try to become a European writer. His sources of income were still mainly English, though: he funded the writing of commercially unsuccessful novels like *The Foot of Clive* and *Corker's Freedom* by travelling up to Manchester to make programmes for Granada TV. One of these, *Before My Time* was an interview with Joe Roberts, born in 1890 to a mining family of thirteen children, ten of whom had died before adulthood.

The Roberts family had sand on the floor instead of carpets, shared beds and an oil lamp. At work, they still ripped the coal out of the earth by hand. Joe started down at fourteen. It was 'the quietest programme on television' according to *The Sunday Times*. 'Still, time-suspended, possessed of a marvellous dignity and severity of line.' The historian Eric Hobsbawm wrote to tell Berger it was 'one of the best programmes I've ever seen on TV, and the general sparseness and economy of the technique was immensely impressive'. Granada forwarded Berger letters of thanks from people who had seen their own working-class experience televised for the first time. From Sheffield, a Mrs Skidmore wrote to describe losing her husband at thirty-seven at the Woodburn Road end of the Nunnery Colliery. To bear out Roberts' point of how little such work was worth she sent him her copy of the colliery's price list.

While working in Manchester Berger also went back to the Forest of Dean. There were coalfields nearby, but the locals, the 'foresters', mostly worked in 'small workshops, quarries, a wood-processing factory, a jam factory, a brickworks'. It might seem odd to talk about geographical remoteness in a country as small as England, Berger admitted, but the centralisation of economic power had 'turned what were once large, vital towns, like Bolton or Rochdale or Wigan, into remote backwaters'. Working with the photographer Jean Mohr, he portrayed the area of the Forest of Dean in *A Fortunate Man: The Story of a Country Doctor* (1967). The way Mohr and Berger worked had something of Orwell and Zola to it. But the way the lightly fictionalised Dr John Sassall has earned his community's trust in the book was more like Josef Herman. By exchanging different forms of 'recognition' with his patients the doctor became, in Berger's phrase, 'the clerk of the foresters' records'.

A Fortunate Man is, among other things, a book about the smallness of English cultural life: the narrow horizons and opportunities it offered ordinary people. In 1968 there briefly looked to be hope of change from a moment of revolutions around the world. Even if they did not succeed, Berger's first response, 'The Nature of Mass Demonstrations', suggested viewing history as a pattern of repeating moments – 'rehearsals' of revolutionary awareness – in which the failures of one era could be drawn on in another. In the face of any mass demonstration, he wrote, power was forced to reveal itself: either as weak, by doing nothing, or as undemocratic by crushing it.

From 1968 Berger traced a line back to 1848 via a demonstration in Milan in 1898 he was researching for his next book: *G.: A Novel*. Sections of *G.* also reappeared in the work which made Berger most famous, the TV series *Ways of Seeing*, produced and directed by Mike Dibb. The programme was first broadcast on BBC2 on 8 January 1972, the night before the National Union of Mineworkers went out on their first official strike since 1926. This time they won: seven weeks later they went back to work, having improved their pay. A second strike in 1974 fatally weakened Edward Heath's Conservative Government.

Throughout *Ways of Seeing*, Berger is wearing a wallpaper-like gold-and-cream shirt to make him stand out against the blue background. It looks pretty garish to anyone watching on YouTube, but to BBC2 viewers that night it would have seemed restrained. They'd just been watching a scene set in a busily patterned nineteenth-century drawing room: a delegation of miners had just announced their strike to a mine shareholder; his wife had disgustedly asked that the windows be opened to clear their smell. This was the second episode of a TV adaptation of *Germinal*. Elsewhere in the Rougon-Macquart series, *La Bête humaine* looks at the rail network which connected the country at unprecedented speeds, *La Terre* at the still-peasant farmers who fed it, and *La Curée* at the financial speculation which sat on top of the whole thing. *Germinal* looked at the energy which powered it all: coal. The basic conflict of the book is between the people who hack it out of the earth and the people who profit from it. There are subdivisions, though: increasingly radical young autodidact Étienne Lantier, the older, more moderate Rasseneur and the ruthless anarchist Souvarine on one side; the hands-on mine owner Deneulin and the abstract speculator Grégoire – he of the drawing room – on the other.

This TV version, adapted by David Turner, kept the action in the nineteenth century but transposed it to the English Midlands. The miners are attempting Black Country accents with varying levels of success, and Étienne is a southern interloper. First broadcast in 1970, it was part of the resources available to people taking the Open University's course on 'The Nineteenth-Century Novel and Its Legacy'. Arnold Kettle, the OU's first professor of literature, flew to Geneva to persuade Berger to contribute to the course, taking his producer, the Irish writer Nuala O'Faolain.

It was a busy year. That November, Berger was awarded the *Guardian* and Booker McConnell Prizes for *G.*, the novel from which many of *Ways of Seeing*'s insights about power, race and class had been adapted. Booker McConnell had by then diversified into financial speculation and the cash and carry trade, but the root of the business was Caribbean sugar plantations using enslaved labour. In a speech at London's Café Royal, Berger recalled the statue in *G.* of a Medici prince flanked by four African figures in chains: an image of the violence and subjugation behind European wealth. He could not straightforwardly accept the money to fund his next project – a study of European migrant labour with Jean Mohr, which was to become the book *A Seventh Man* – so he would share it with the London chapter of the Black Panthers. He was, he reminded one interviewer, a revolutionary writer.

Rather than go back home after the speech, Berger got the train up to the mining town of Creswell, which O'Faolain had chosen for their Zola programme. Coal production had started there in 1897. The mine was the site of Derbyshire's worst mining disaster – a fire started by a conveyor belt in 1950 – but also of a model village with accommodation and facilities for the workers. In her memoir *Are You Somebody* O'Faolain describes the brief affair she and Berger had on set, and their struggles with the material. The way through, as so often with Berger's work, was an image: a photograph of Zola in his home, as 'overstuffed' as the Grégoires': a counterpoint to the story of him visiting a mine in Anzin to get the detail of the book right.

As Berger put it in the final script, both he and Zola are writers with 'strong working-class sympathies, trying to give some idea to someone who's never been near a mine, what's involved in working in one'. But there is an unbridgeable gap, not in friendliness, but in experience, which could only be closed by a life spent actually doing the work. On the film, the gap is emphasised, or even enacted by the separateness between Berger's studio voiceover and the footage of him in the pit, dressed in National Coal Board overalls.

As a political novel, *Germinal* can be ambivalent. Berger thought Zola was 'dynamically confused' in the face of the exploitation he saw, so that the book 'sometimes outstrips or even contradicts his intentions'. Karl Marx is mentioned, though among the thinkers Étienne has read but not really understood. The mine owners give their perspective too, explaining that they are simply doing their best in the economic circumstances they find themselves in; it is for the reader to observe the feasts they enjoy while their workers starve. But the novel nevertheless became an icon of left-wing thought. 'Germinal! Germinal! Germinal!' was chanted at Zola's vast funeral in 1902, and, in life, he agreed with every request to reprint it to help socialist journals build their circulation. The title, suggestive of something sprouting beneath the earth, was the name of the seventh month in the new calendar established after the 1789 French Revolution. By the time Zola was writing a century later, he had already lived through several attempts to revive its spirit, including the 1871 Paris Commune. It squares exactly with what Berger meant by the rehearsals in 'The Nature of Mass Demonstrations'.

Berger and O'Faolain's film had a different production team to *Ways of Seeing* – Henry Farrar on camera, Malcolm Webberly on sound, Michael Graham-Smith on graphic design and editing by Des Murphy – but it's recognisably from the same moment of left-wing television-making. It uses the techniques *Ways of Seeing* had encouraged viewers to be sceptical of, changing the meaning of images by overlaying sound and text, and juxtaposing them in sequence through the techniques of montage.

Like *Germinal*, the film tries to take in what a social scientist would call the life-world of Creswell. It shows some of the same workers among their wives and families, playing snooker and bingo, and drinking in the club. In the hall, Berger watches a boy training up to be part of the village brass band, and the rehearsal for a fruity-sounding music-hall number, 'Here We Are, Here We Are, Here We Are Again'. A decent part of the TV audience would still have recognised the song as a Great War standard, written by Charles Knight and Kenneth Lyle in 1914. The camera cuts to an elderly man with a moustache and liver spots. The distance between the jauntiness of the tune and the sadness of his gaze suggests that he remembers it from the first time around.

It's an eloquent piece of editing. *G.* had been, among other things, a novel about what Berger called 'The Moment of Cubism' (1907–1914); and the way it immediately preceded European nations treating their own populations in the same way they had long treated those of their colonies. The theory that industrialised, racialised mass murder in nineteenth-century European colonies led to industrialised, racialised mass murder in twentieth-century Europe has been described as the 'imperial boomerang'. One proponent of the theory was the poet Aimé Césaire, whose *Cahier d'un retour au pays natal* (1938) Berger and his partner and collaborator Anya Berger had translated in 1969. (Anya, a key influence on the Women's Liberation aspects of *Ways of Seeing* had also worked as Anna Bostock, and done translation work for the Coal Board which meant she could help with the terminology.)

A few frames later, though, Berger's *Germinal* is making an inverse, but related, point. The situation is not the same, in British and European mines, as it was in the nineteenth century. 'The absolute degree of exploitation which Zola saw continues,' Berger argues, over newsreel footage of what appears to be South African mines. Work as dehumanising as nineteenth-century mining still goes on to make British and European standards of life possible. It is just even further out of sight. For a writer like Berger, the only response is solidarity in the face of a power which is only concerned with profit.

In the image of Berger underground watching people work, there is the seed of his later writing about cave paintings and political hope. More immediately, the Berger of *Germinal* is well on the way to *A Seventh Man*, not just in the montage of text and image, or in the relation of what were then called the Third and First Worlds. 'Despite all his claims to be scientific, despite all his research, *Germinal* is essentially a book about a dream,' Berger's voiceover argues. This dream, often a nightmare, 'was born out of what Zola could not know about his subject matter. And into that space, into that gap, which disturbed him profoundly, he projected his conscious and his unconscious fears and hopes.'

For a twentieth-century audience used to the theories of Sigmund Freud, it seems obvious to interpret *Germinal*'s world of sex, murder and dark body-swallowing tunnels through the frame of the unconscious. Berger would become increasingly interested in the idea that, rather than just a site of past trauma, dreams can also be a way of imagining a different future. This sense of hope is stronger in the *Germinal* film than in *A Seventh Man*.

Berger later described the post-1968 period as one of 'normalisation', a global political stasis in which things might be exchanged but not fundamentally changed. For the National Union of Miners, though, the early seventies had been so much a moment of victory that the Conservative MP Nicholas Ridley drew up a strategy for crushing the unions the next time they went out on strike. On 3 March 1984, this happened in response to the Thatcher government's programme of pit closures.

According to 'The Nature of Mass Demonstrations', crowds face the state with a choice between 'displayed weakness and displayed authoritarianism'. On 18 June 1984, the British state set the stage for a display of its own authoritarianism. Pickets were directed by police to the Coking Plant at Orgreave, South Yorkshire, and subjected to a cavalry charge. Ninety-five pickets – who could have worn protective work clothing if they'd been preparing for violence, as the police claimed, but wore T-shirts and trainers instead – were prosecuted. In the evening news, the BBC showed reversed footage, giving the false impression that the pickets attacked first.

A month later, at midnight on 17 July 1984, Berger and O'Faolain's *Germinal* film was shown again on BBC2. By then, Berger was living between Paris and the village of Quincy in the French Alps. On his return to England, he was asked what Anthony Barnett, a friend whom Berger had consulted about what to do with the Booker Prize, called the 'inevitable' question: why he wasn't back in the country of his birth fighting Thatcherism. He was working on a project closer to Zola's *La Terre*: *Into Their Labours*, a series of stories about the decline of peasant life around the world, particularly in the face of the economic policies Thatcher and Reagan enforced. Rather than visiting like a Zola or an Orwell, he was living there like a Herman.

In 1987, Berger told Eva Figes in private that he thought there were 'very few occasions when political assassination serves any purpose at all, except to encourage further oppression. But I think Thatcher supplies such an occasion . . .' His fullest public statement on the subject was 'Miners', a text to accompany a 1989 exhibition by the Swedish artists Knud and Solwei Stampe in Middlesbrough. In 2019, the artist Emily Hesse and the writer Martyn Hudson arranged a symposium testifying to the show's lasting impact on the area. Further afield, its legacy is one of Berger's clearest statements on the power of art, rooted in his sense that what linked communities like Creswell with Quincy was the way Thatcher's neoliberalism aimed to cut off their resistance by cutting off their sense of history.

Hudson pointed out the connections with the imagery of *Germinal* in the 2019 commemoration, and, in the image of 'the Goliath police with their bloody truncheons', there are obvious echoes of the recent memory of Orgreave, specific mentions of 'sleepless nights during the last few years in Scotland and South Wales, Derbyshire and Kent, Yorkshire, Northumberland', and deeper memories of the state wanting to break 'your inheritance, your skills, your communities, your poetry, your clubs, your home and, wherever possible, your bones too'. But Berger, who had lost his Chilean friend Orlando Letelier to a car bomb in 1976, was also thinking of Thatcher's friend General Augusto Pinochet. 'The avenging heroes,' he writes, still in *Germinal* mode, 'are now being dreamt up and awaited.'

Germinal has not been on television for decades. A document, as Berger admits, is always an outsider's view. Joe Roberts would agree that there is nothing to be mourned in the sort of work it shows, but it stands partly as a document of the communities or life-worlds killed off and not replaced by Thatcherism. Anthony Barnett once described Henry Moore's work as 'an authentic expression of the special tragedy of the civilian population in the long war that began as Moore's father was taken from the fields to the mines, and which still continues as it hurtles us towards unknown destinations'.

Watching it now, or seeing it laid out on a page on the fortieth anniversary of Orgreave, it's clearer what these unknown destinations are: environmental degradation, scarred land, choked skies, global warming. Because the focus on profit survives, so do nineteenth-century mining conditions, where Congolese children dig cobalt so richer people thousands of miles away can continue to live the same lifestyles, only with battery-powered cars. Berger considered *The Underground Sea* as a title because it has the same sense of unpredictable energy, bursting from below the ground. Now the sense of unleashing prehistoric energy has a different set of meanings. Climate change was not one of Berger's great themes, but in 2002 he wondered how many Americans agreed with 'George W. Bush's withdrawal from the Kyoto Protocol over the carbon-dioxide greenhouse effect, which is already provoking disastrous floods in many places and threatens, within the next twenty-five years, far worse disasters?'

On the anniversary of the 1984 Miners' Strikes, the number of days being lost to industrial action in the UK has returned to levels not seen since the eighties. For Eddie Dempsey of the Rail, Maritime and Transport Union, all this is a reminder that 'there isn't a train that moves in this country, not a bin gets emptied, or a shelf stacked without the kind permission of the working class'. The UK Government, meanwhile, is passing new policing acts to limit freedoms of protest and political expression, defining demonstrations as 'disruption to the life of the community'.

Elements of *Germinal*'s form have dated, but it still presents its viewers with a set of questions about how to work with the past. They seem particularly worth asking in a year where archive footage of the violence of Orgreave will be replayed across platforms and feeds. This book tries to follow the meaning and spirit of Berger's film by staying close to its pairing of image and text. Still, adapting something from film to page is a conscious re-versioning. Split-second clips turn to portraits and panning shots are set into landscapes, allowing the viewer to stray from Berger and bring Creswell and its people into the foreground. This, too, is a way of seeing bound up with a moment in history: much of the recent writing about the strike has focused as much on what it felt like being part of a mining community as on the political background.

As the *Germinal* film closes, Berger connects the intertwined images of recurring dreams and revolutions to Zola's title, and the seasons of the earth. 'Where is the harvest of a future age?'

he asks. From a little girl running to a miner at work, a sample of humanity comes up on screen. Against some of these images, he repeats: 'Exploitation. Exploitation.' But then repeats, a little later: 'Alive. Alive. Alive.' If there is hope of change, he argues, it comes from 'the unfinished and unpredictable energy of people.'

Miners
1989

When the just cause is defeated, when the courageous are humiliated, when men proven at pit bottom and pit head are treated like trash, when nobility is shat upon, and the judges in court believe lies, and slanderers are paid to slander with salaries which might keep alive the families of a dozen miners on strike, when the Goliath police with their bloody truncheons find themselves not in the dock but on the Honours List, when our past is dishonoured and its promises and sacrifices shrugged off with ignorant and evil smiles, when whole families come to suspect that those who wield power are deaf to reason and every plea, and that there is no appeal anywhere, when gradually you realise that, whatever words there may be in the dictionary, whatever the Queen says or parliamentary correspondents report, whatever the system calls itself to mask its shamelessness and egoism, when gradually you realise that They are out to break you, out to break your inheritance, your skills, your communities, your poetry, your clubs, your home and, wherever possible, your bones too, when people finally realise this, they may also hear, striking in their head, the hour of assassinations, of justified vengeance. On sleepless nights during the last few years in Scotland and South Wales, Derbyshire and Kent, Yorkshire, Northumberland and Lancashire, many, as they lay reflecting on their beds, heard, I am sure, this hour striking. And nothing could be more human, more tender than such a proposed vision of the pitiless being summarily executed by the pitiful. It is the word 'tender' which we cherish and which They can never understand, for they do not know what it refers to. This vision is occurring all over the world. The avenging heroes are now being dreamt up and awaited. They are already feared by the pitiless and blessed by me and maybe by you.

I would shield any such hero to my fullest capacity. Yet if, during the time I was sheltering him, he told me he liked drawing, or, supposing it was a woman, she told me she'd always wanted to paint, and had never had the chance or the time to do so, if this happened, then I think I'd say: Look, if you want to, it's possible you may achieve what you are setting out to do in another way, a way less likely to fall out on your comrades and less open to confusion. I can't tell you what art does and how it does it, but I know that often art has judged the judges, pleased revenge to the innocent and shown to the future what the past has suffered, so that it has never been forgotten. I know too that the powerful fear art, whatever its form, when it does this, and that amongst the people such art sometimes runs like a rumour and a legend because it makes sense of what life's brutalities cannot, a sense that unites us, for it is inseparable from a justice at last. Art, when it functions like this, becomes a meeting-place of the invisible, the irreducible, the enduring, guts, and honour.

Germinal

1972

By 1884 Zola was rich and successful.
He wrote his novels in a villa near Paris.

He knew he wanted to write a novel about a miners' strike.
Such a strike broke out in northern France.
He went there for a week and informed himself.
He went back to his villa near Paris and wrote *Germinal*.

GERMINAL
discussed by JOHN BERGER

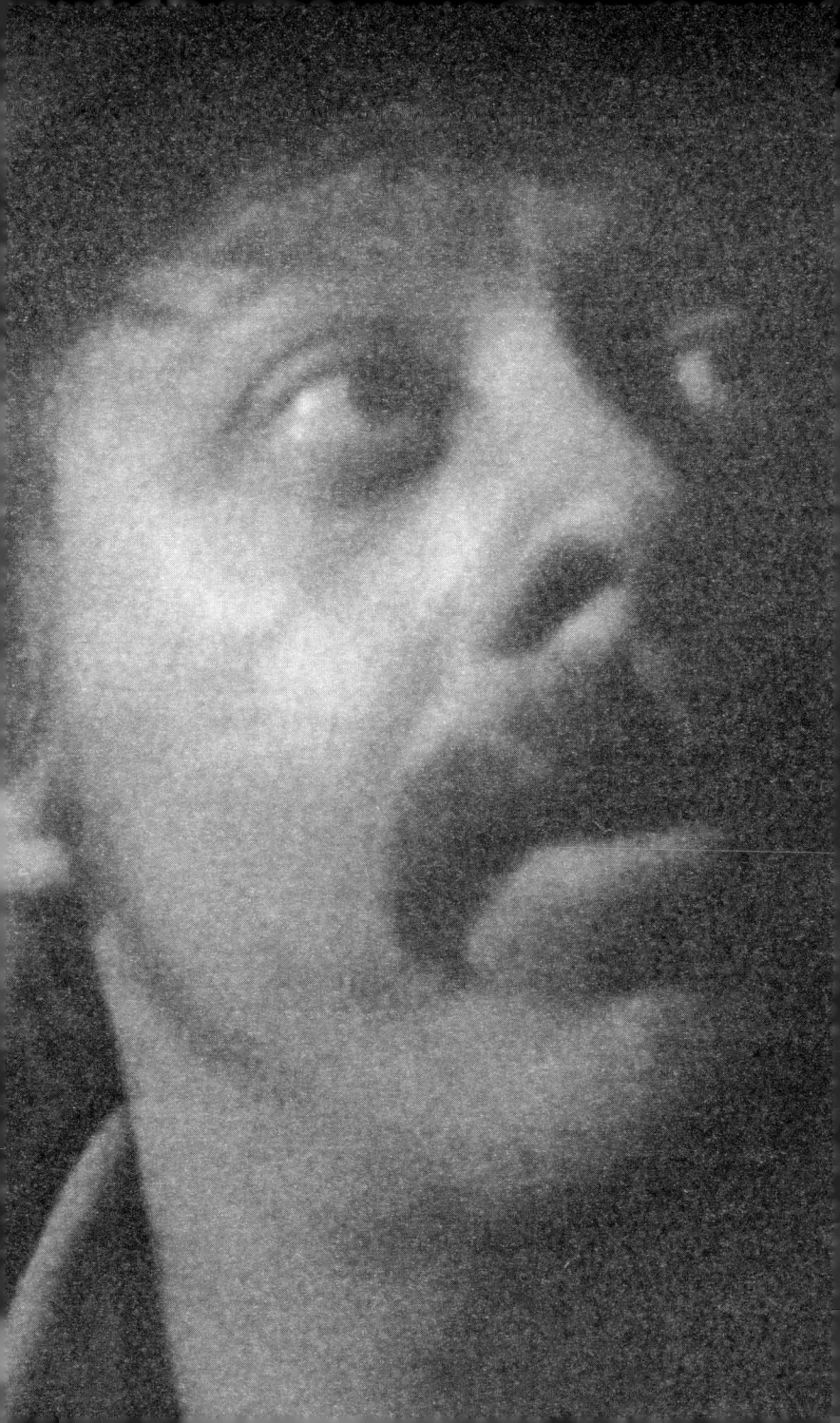

I had been down a mine four times.
These Derbyshire miners 400 or 4,000 times.

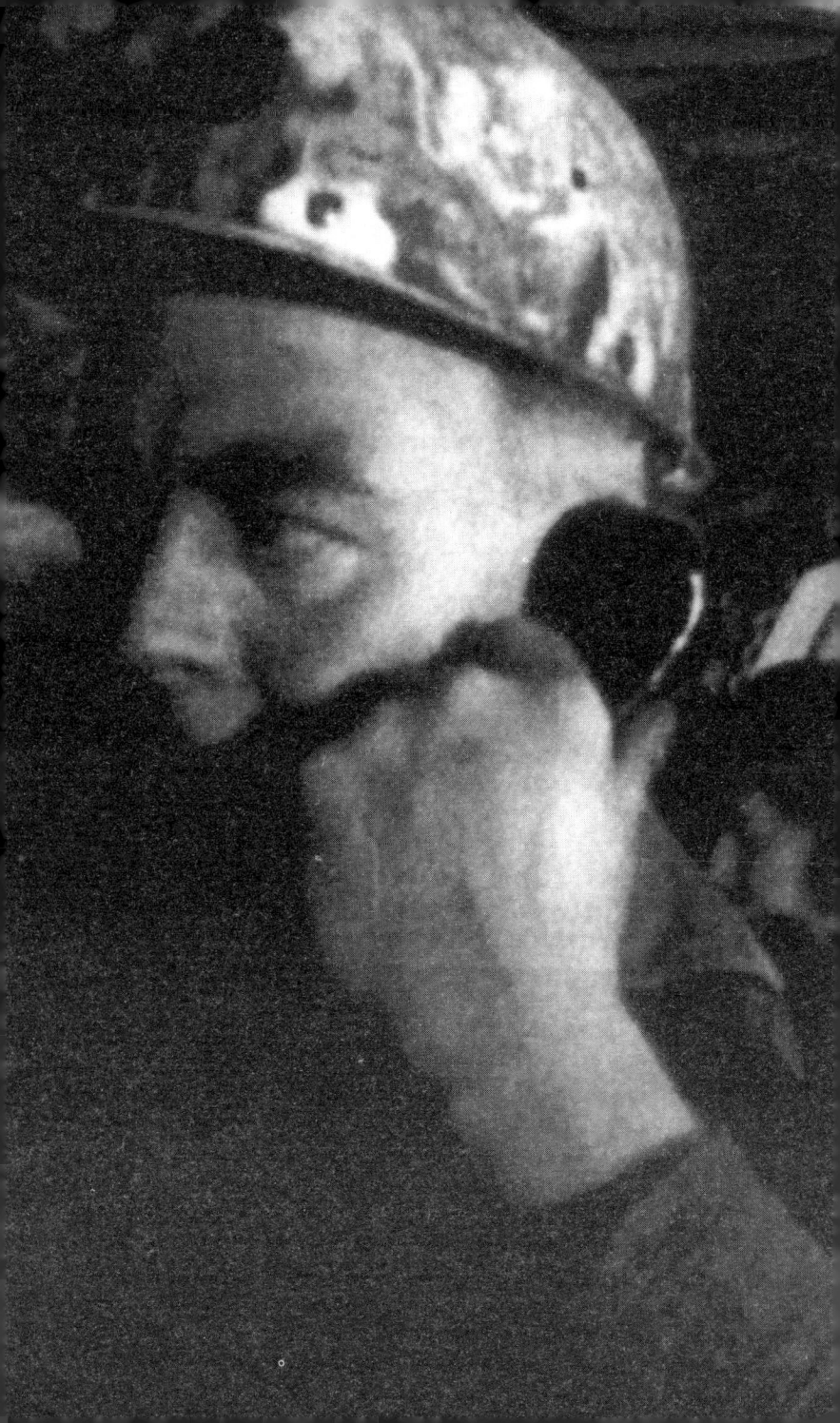

At pit bottom, the atmosphere is not unlike a ship's engine room. There's no sense of the nature of the earth you're in and under.

The whitewash on the walls somehow gives the semblance of still being above ground. But the whitewash only lasts for about twenty yards. And where the whitewash stops, so does the memory of fresh air.

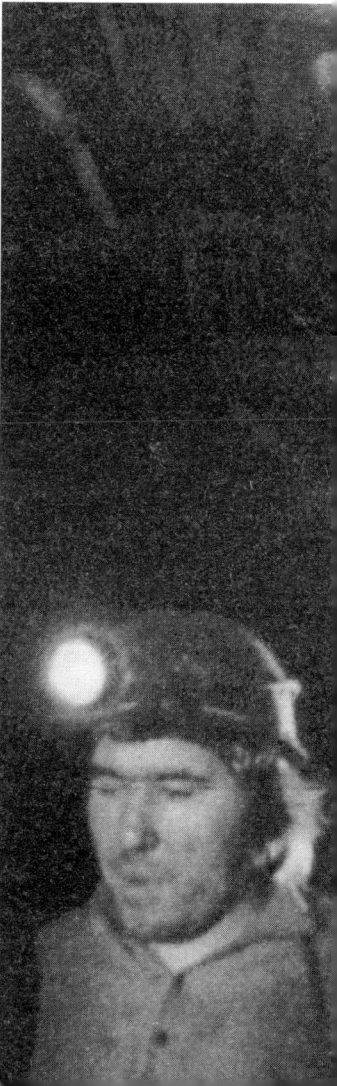

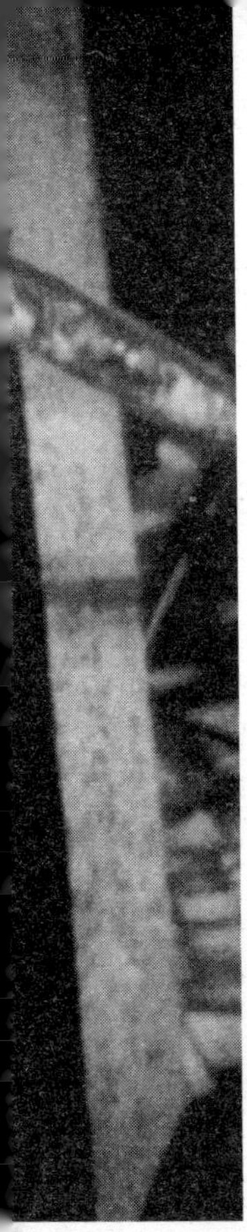

The coalface, where they're going to work, is about a mile away. It's only when you're swimming out to sea that like now you carry with you, just underneath your mind, the distance back.

As you walk away, there's less and less space for your body, until under the lip at the cold face, only the coal-cutting machine can go on, gouging out coal, leaving space where the coal was.

In this cramped space, half a mile underground where the air is hot and silted with coal dust, hard work becomes harder, and alertness becomes more alert. The conveyor belt is deceptive; its regularity is not really mechanical. It is the colliers' minute-by-minute achievement against unforeseeable snags.

The coal face is the extremity of the line, and when you crawl out, it's like walking away from an edge.

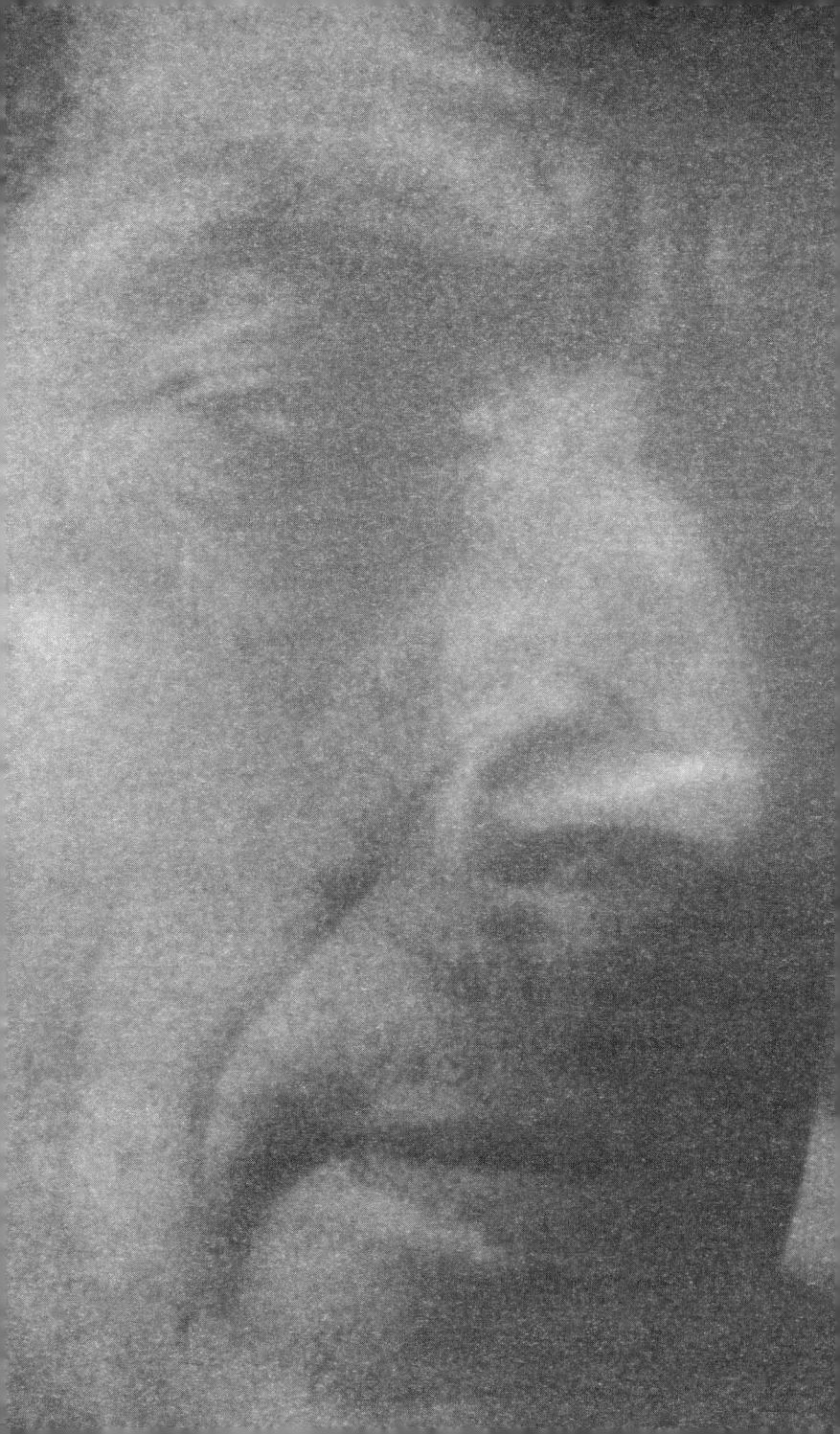

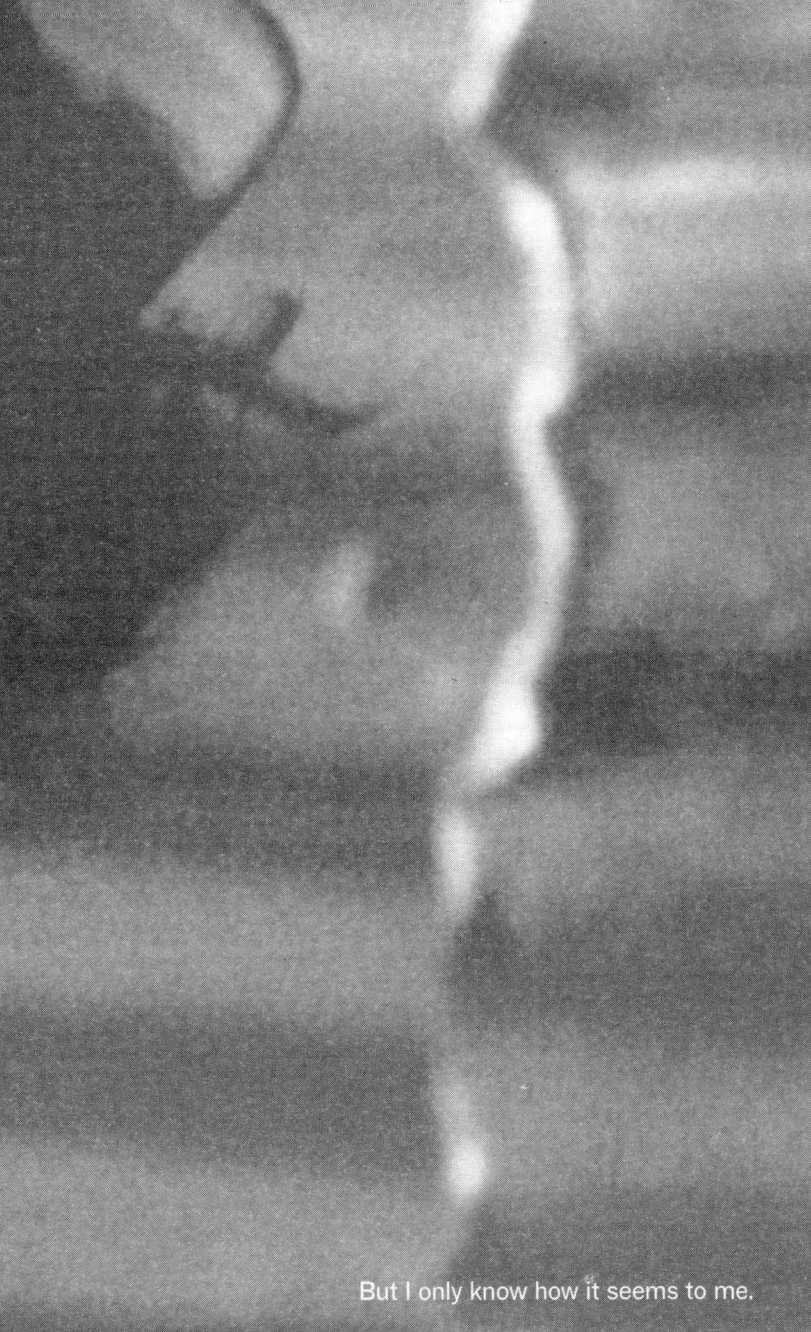

We made that bit of film underground. To give some idea of what working in a mine is like. Sometimes over the film you heard my voice describing my own impressions.

Very roughly, and very briefly, I was in the same kind of situation as Zola.

A writer with strong working-class sympathies trying to give some idea to someone who's never been near a mine what's involved in working in one.

At a little, we may have achieved our aim. But I think that bit of film also demonstrated something else. It demonstrated the gap which exists between the miners and myself.

I don't mean a gap in terms of talk or friendliness; I mean a gap in terms of experience. And the only way of closing that gap would be to work down a pit. Here or elsewhere. Visiting is not enough. Reading isn't enough. Imagination isn't enough.

A large part of the miner's life remains mysterious to me. I am ignorant.

And as a writer, I cannot overcome that ignorance. The only way of overcoming it would be to become a miner. And this is true. Even though today we may drive the same kind of car, eat the same sort of food, watch the same television programmes. This is a limitation, which the techniques of documentary tend to ignore.

A document is always an outsider's view.

Even if my documentation of this village in its life was as exact and brilliant as Zola's, there'd still be a gap.

When we were making this film, the people of Creswell didn't give a damn about the camera. They know who they are without any outsider confirming it.

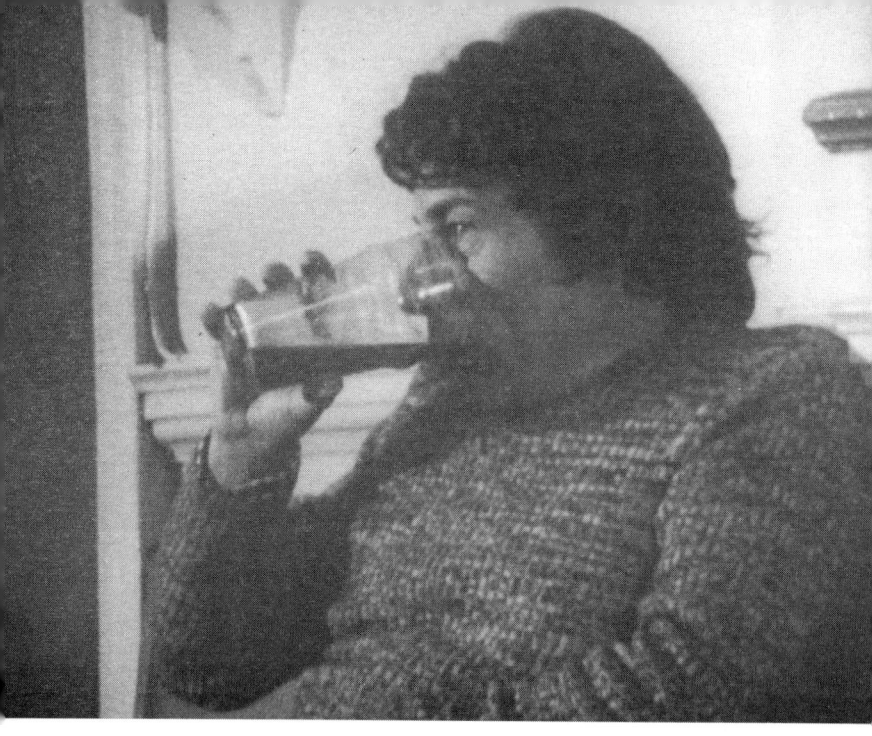

Everyone in this village is connected because the mine and its history is as familiar to them as the weather.

Here we are, here we are, here we are again
There's Pat and Mac, and Tommy and Jack and Joe
When there's trouble brewing, when there's something doing
Are we downhearted? NO, let them all come
Here we are, here we are, here we are again
Fit and well and feeling as right as rain
Never mind the weather, now then, all together
Hello, hello, here we are again.

Charles Knight and Kenneth Lyle (1914)

As to what other people dream, we can only speculate.
Is there a man or woman in this village who has not
dreamt, when they are asleep, of the pit?

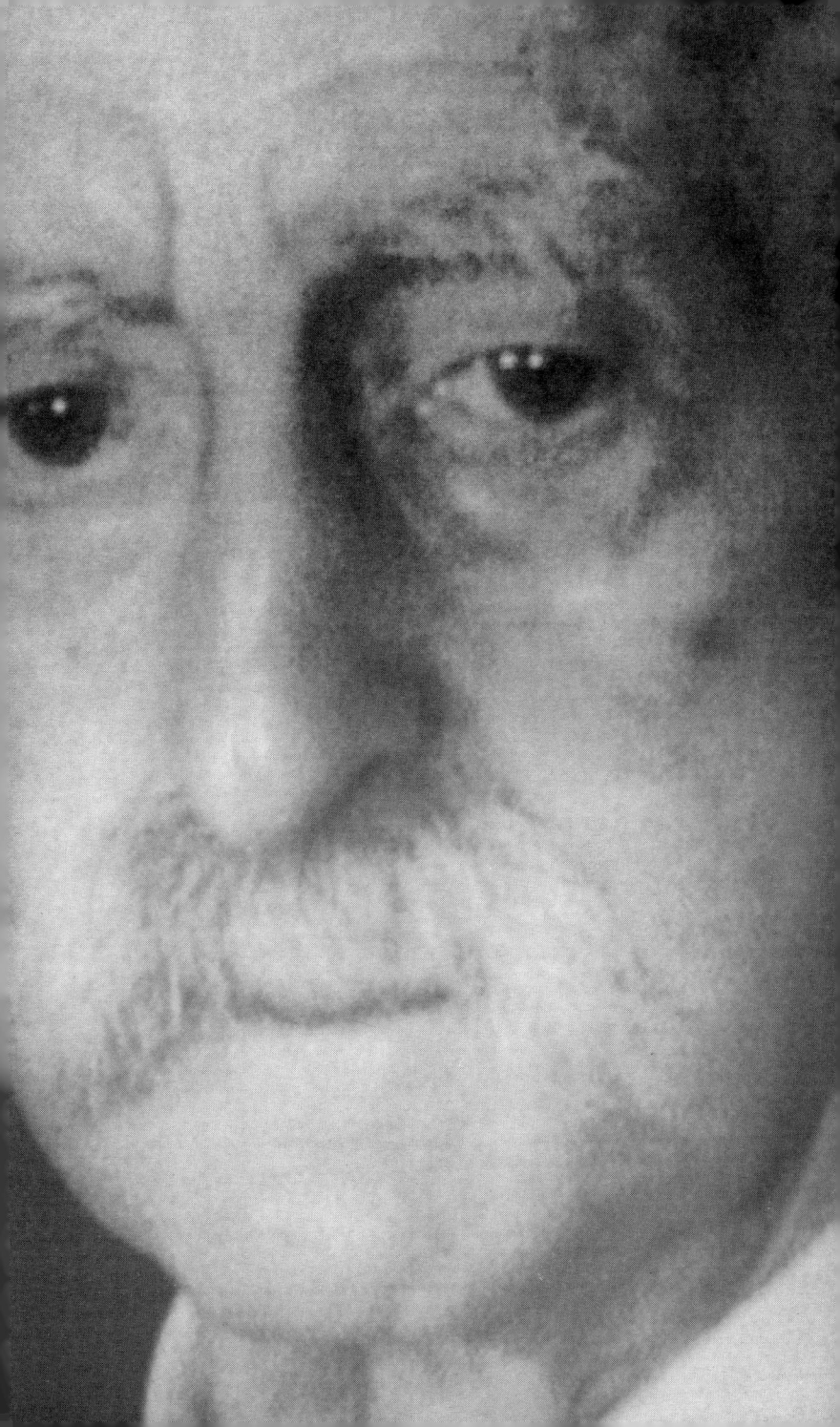

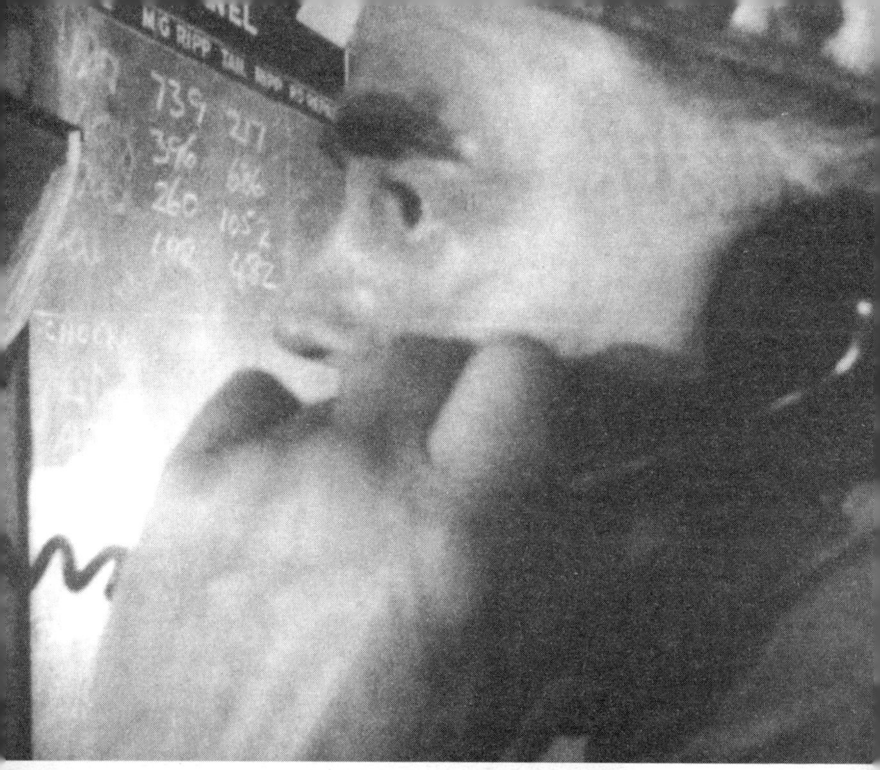

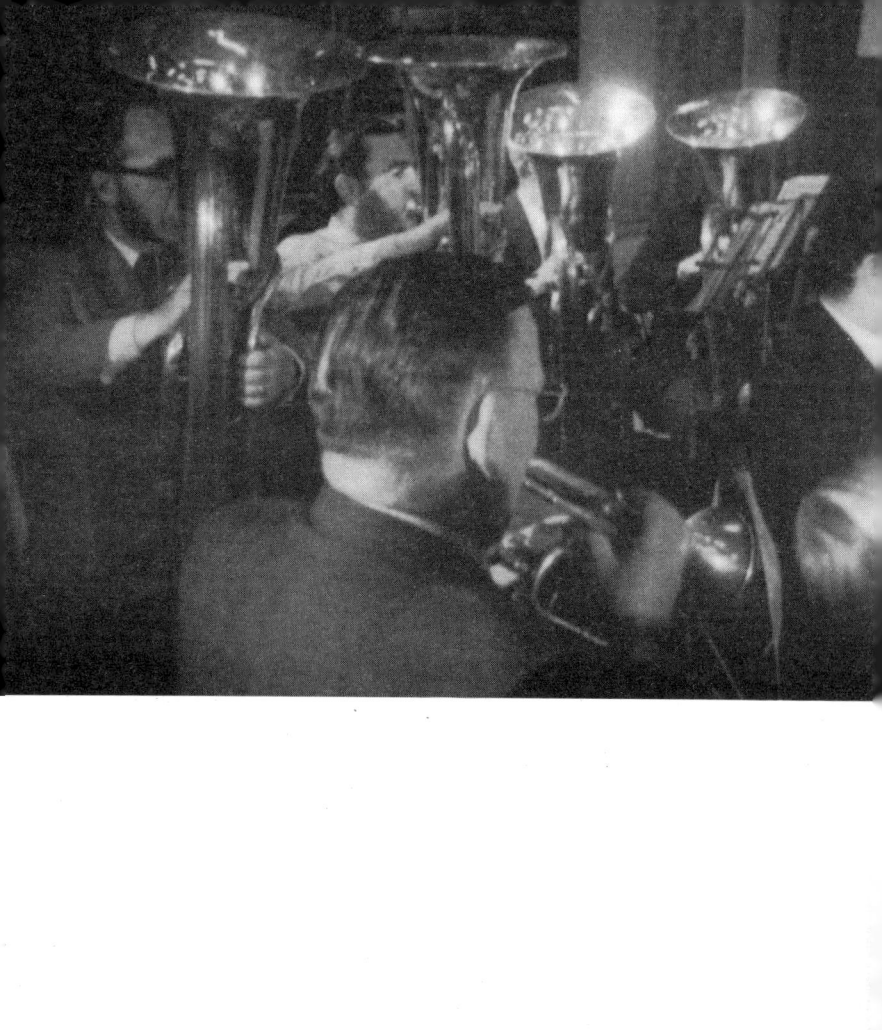

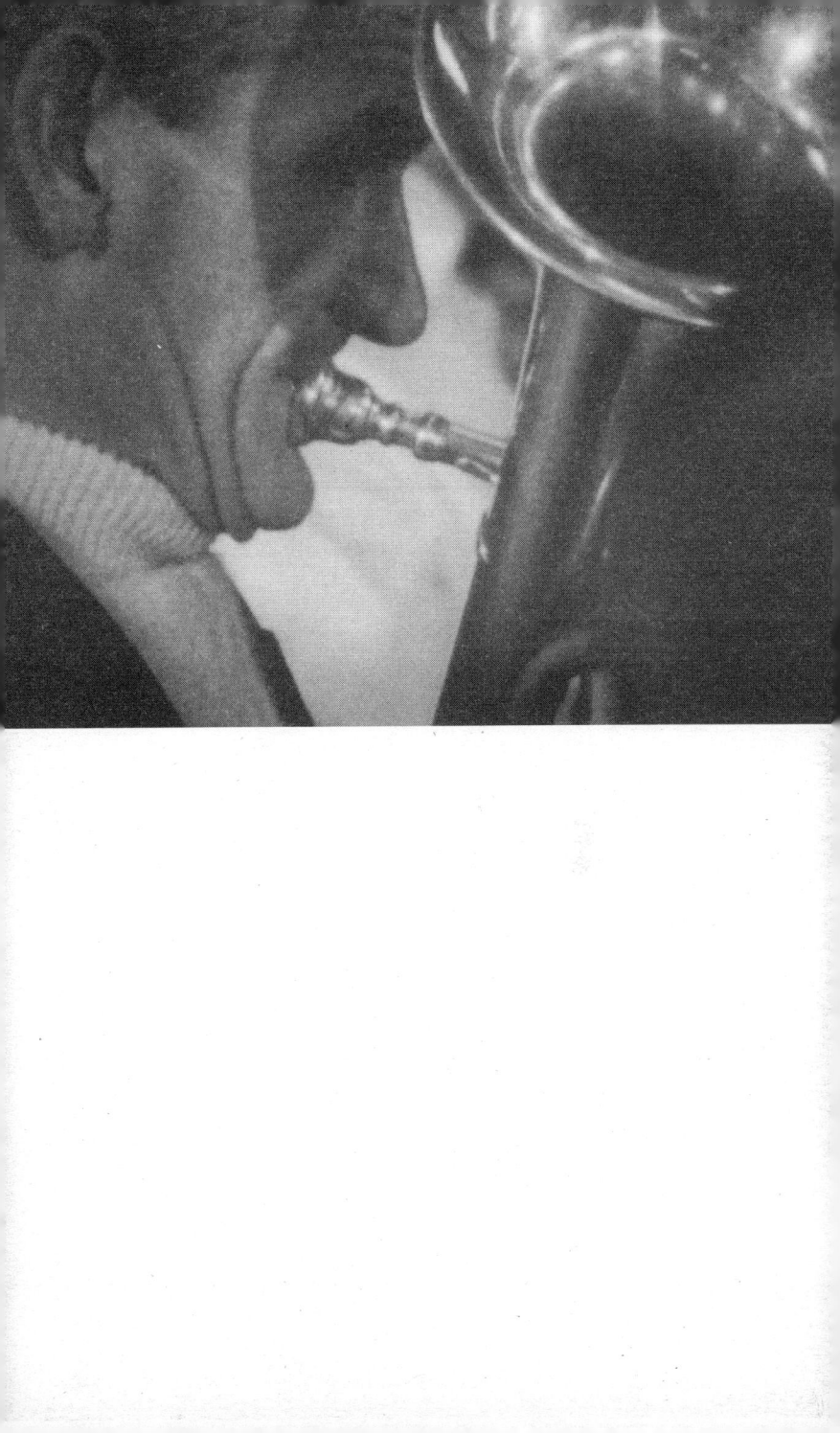

For Zola, because of the extremity of the poverty and injustice he was witnessing, this gap, this mysterious aspect of a miner's life, was much more blatant. And at the level of his imagination, he recognised this.

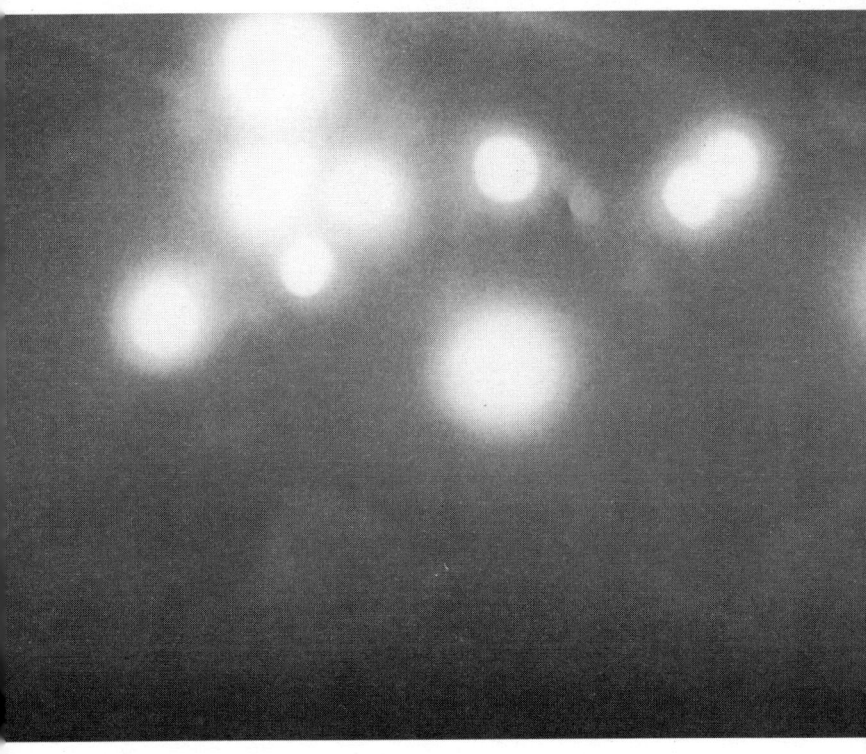

Despite all his claims to be scientific, despite all his research, *Germinal* is essentially a book about a dream. A dream which is often a nightmare.

It's full of mysterious forces. The power, the fury of the mob. The madness of the old man at the end. Étienne's hereditary violence. The underground sea that floods the mine. The underground fire. And this dream, which was often a nightmare, was born out of what Zola could not know about his subject matter. And into that space, into that gap, which disturbed him profoundly, he projected his conscious and his unconscious fears and hopes.

I don't want to interpret the whole novel according to this theory. But the main elements, the principal spectres of this dream-nightmare are clear enough. They are there in the title. A new world is germinating underneath the ground. And when it arrives, it will crack open the earth.

And Zola, his intuition was that this world would be one of justice and equality.

Meanwhile, there are, present, spectres and dreams. There's the lyric dream of the animal life, according to Zola, of the free sexuality of village 240. The vision of this dream provoked Monsieur Hennebeau to say that he would exchange all his social and economic privilege for the sake of participating in it.

But overriding all, there is the spectre of the mob. The mass avenging their hunger. And the suffering that they've experienced, by destroying everything that they can lay their hands on.

And then there's a kind of subsidiary spectre – anarchism, as embodied in Souvarine. This in the end, is the agent along with the underground sea, of the destruction of the mine.

And that last part of the book, in the flooded mine, has all the exact quality of a dream.
   Where the whole of life is summarised in single images.

What I'm saying is that all this happens in *Germinal* as in no other work by Zola because his researches, his investigations, his visits brought him to the edge of an unbridgeable abyss.

The abyss between the condition of his own life as a writer and the condition of the lives of those he was writing about. And one of the reasons why *Germinal* now is a great book is that Zola realised that in such a context compassion is inadequate.

Of course, the situation is not the same today in a modern mine in Britain or Europe. Though all mining retains many nineteenth century aspects. The gap still exists between visitor and miner. But it's no longer full of the same spectres, because the political situation is not the same.

The absolute degree of exploitation which Zola saw continues.

Exploitation.

It's easy to deceive oneself into thinking that images like those need not affect one's life. For Zola, it was the proximity of the mining proletariat that made his fears and his hopes as deep as the pits themselves.

In his fears, he never altogether escaped the prejudices and way of reasoning of the middle class to which he belonged.

But his hopes were more generous and more universal. Indeed, one might say that he was haunted by his hopes. For it was they, not his fears, which made it impossible for him to merely describe the life he saw around him.

In the face of exploitation, Zola was dynamically confused so that *Germinal* sometimes outstrips or even contradicts his intentions. He intended the book to be a warning to his own class.

> What I wanted to do was to cry out to the privileged people of the world, the masters. Beware. Look under the earth. Look at the wretches who toil and suffer. There may still be time to avoid the final catastrophe.
>
> But make haste to do justice or you will be in peril. The Earth will open and the nation will be swallowed up by one of the most terrible calamities in history.

Yet the end of *Germinal* is not a cry of fear. It moves on and out as if a future justice is pulling the whole world of the book towards itself.

> For if one class had to be devoured surely the people, vigorous and young, must devour the effette and luxury-loving bourgeoisie? A new society needed new blood. In his expectation of a new invasion of barbarians regenerating the decayed nations of the old world, he rediscovered his absolute faith in a coming revolution, and this time it would be the real one, whose fires would cast their red glare over the end of this epoch even as the rising sun was now drenching the sky in blood.

On he walked, lost in these dreams, hitting stones with his Dogwood stick. On looking round, however, he saw the familiar landmarks at the foreshore berth just over there. He remembered taking over command of the crowd on the morning they had stormed the pits. And today, the brutish, deadly, ill-paid toil was beginning all over again. On the other side, he thought he could hear the distant sound of picks very soft, but regular and insistent. Seven hundred metres under the ground. It was his mates, whom he had just seen going down, his black comrades, tapping away in silent rage. To left and to right far away into the distance he thought he could recognise other friends under the corn, the hedges and young trees. The April sun was now well up in the sky, shedding its glorious warming rays on the teeming earth. Life was springing from her fertile womb. Buds were bursting into leaf and the fields were quickening with fresh green grass. Everywhere seeds were swelling and lengthening, cracking open the plain in their upward thrust for warmth and light. The sap was rising in abundance with whispering voices, the germs of life were opening with a kiss.

On and on, ever more insistently, his comrades were tapping, tapping, as though they too were rising through the ground. On this youthful morning in the faraway rays of the sun, the whole country was alive with this sound. Men were springing up, a black, avenging host was slowly germinating in the furrows, thrusting upwards for the harvests of future ages. And very soon their germination would crack the earth asunder.

What does that mean three generations after it was written? Where is the harvest of the future age?

We see that things have changed, improved. What is nineteenth-century prophecy to us now? It is everywhere potent and especially in the working class, most especially perhaps among miners.

The aspirations of the past, which thrust through *Germinal*, cannot be written off unless they have been achieved. Which is not the case. The desire to be free and equal coexists with the actual situation of a modern miner's life always, and most evidently when they strike.

Germinal lives because Zola knew the dimension of hope, which was and is inseparable from the fact of being a worker. Zola's novel is now part of our knowledge of the world.

And in a mining village it reminds us of the unfinished and unpredictable energy of people.

Alive.

Alive.

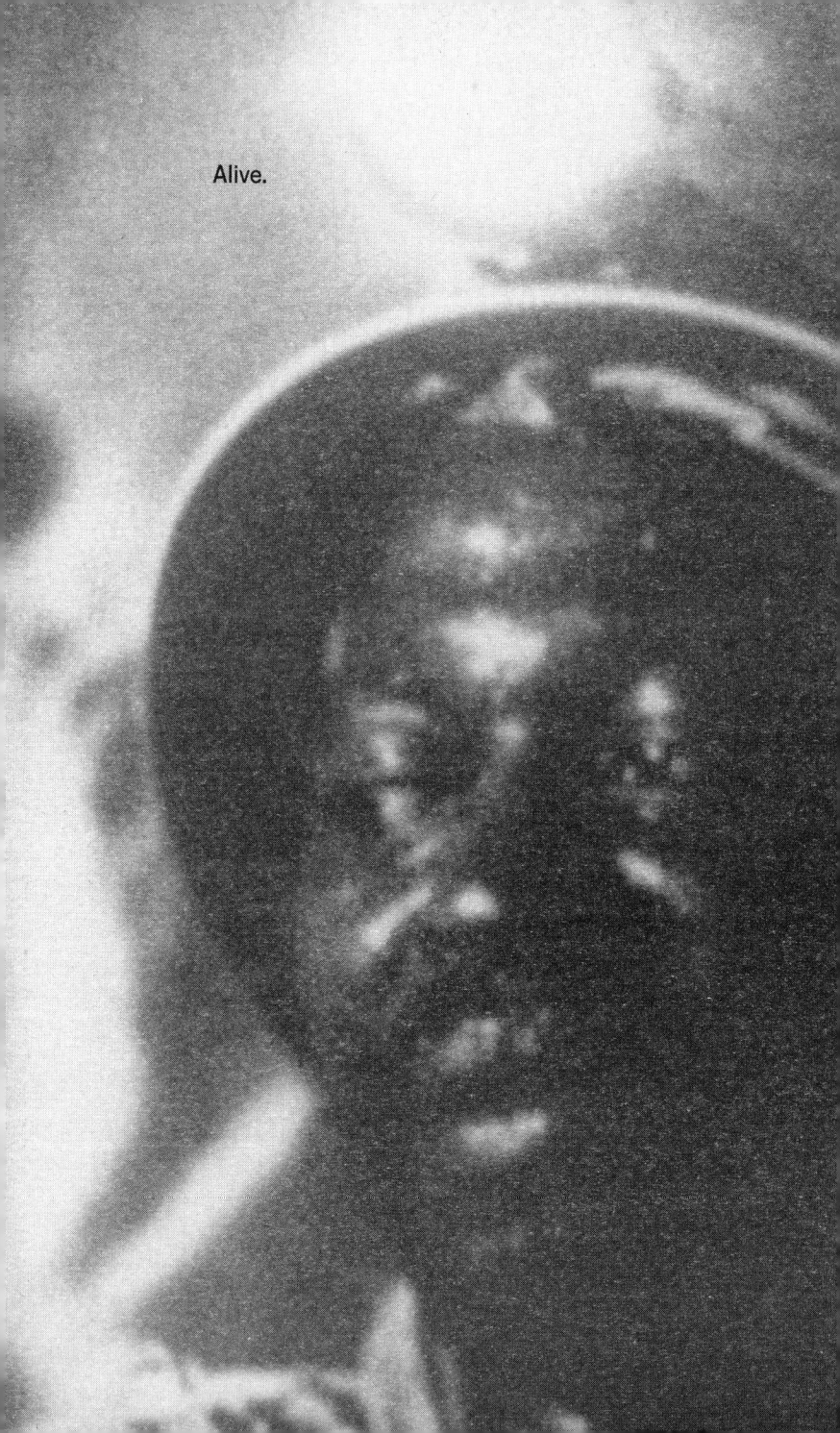

Alive.

Before My Time
*Interview between John Berger and Joe Roberts,
Script for Transmission, 11 July 1963*

Continuity voiceover: *The world before the 1914 war, Queen Victoria's Diamond Jubilee and the long Edwardian summer. The British Empire extended over almost a quarter of the world; Britain still exported more goods than any other country. But what was it like to make the goods? What was it like to be a northern industrial worker in those days? The basis of our industrial power was, then, coal; we were also exporting more coal than ever before or since. Over one million men were employed in the mining industry; their average wage was eighty pounds a year. Coal owners' profits averaged twenty million pounds a year. Joe Roberts was a miner at that time; he is talking now with John Berger.*

John Berger: Tell me, when were you born and where?
   Joe Roberts: I was born in Swinton in 1890.

B: And your father was a miner?
   R: Yes.

B: How many were in the family?
R: Thirteen.

B: Yes.
R: My mother had thirteen children.

B: Brother and sisters?
R: Yes.

B: Did they become miners?
R: No. Only my brother. He's dead now. He was a miner and then he started up on his own.

B: What happened to the others then?
R: Well, they died. And they died, and I suppose in those days . . .

B: How many of them died?
R: Ten.

B: All as children?
R: Yes.

B: What of?
R: I couldn't tell you. I am only guessing that, well, it might have been malnutrition or it might not, but it was one of those things. They didn't live. Ten died.

B: Do you remember any of them dying yourself?
R: Yes. I remember them, yes. I have a faint memory. Not a great memory of them. But the ten died and only three of us lived. My sisters and two brothers. One brother and me. And my brother died.

B: What sort of house did you live in then?

R: Two down and one up. There was only one bedroom and two places down.

B: And how many would be in the family?

R: Well then, there was . . . how many children? I should say about five in the family.

B: How did you sleep then?

R: Oh. The best way we could.

B: Which was?

R: Well, sleep in the same room as my parents.

B: Did you have enough beds to go round?

R: Well, yes. And we had no gas in those days. It was an oil lamp and we'd no carpets on the floors. We used to put sand on the floor and sweep it up after it had been down two days. And we never – I've never – lived in a house, until I was married, where there was a matting. Never had a bath. No.

B: What about a lavatory in this house?

R: No. Fifty yards away, You had to walk fifty yards away from it. One lavatory for two families.

B: And how did you heat it?

R: Um?

B: How did you heat the house?

R: Just by coal fire. The ordinary coal fire.

B: What about food?

R: Well, it was rough. We had enough. But it was rough, you know.

B: And your father. What would his wages have been about?

R: In those days I should think me dad was . . . his wages would be about, let me see now . . . he wouldn't be getting above thirty bob a week. No. Thirty bob to thirty-five bob a week.

B: And none of the other family earning at this stage?

R: No, oh no . . . no . . . nobody else was earning anything.

B: Do you remember any piece of furniture for instance or something which the family wanted which you used to save up to try and get?

R: Yes. A sideboard. We never had a sideboard when I was a boy. We had no sideboard. Couldn't afford one.

B: Did you have enough chairs to go round?

R: Yes. We had chairs.

B: So just really the bare bits of furniture.

R: Bare bits of furniture. Just to sit on, and that was all we had.

B: Whilst you were still at school, or even before you were going to school, did you have to do jobs about the house or help?

R: No. No. I didn't. My mother was capable of doing that. But I had done this in the morning before I'd gone to school: I've gone out at six o'clock in the morning with a bucket to pick a bucket full of coal to keep the fire going. Before I've gone to school.

B: Where did you pick it from?

R: I've stood against the . . . I've stood near the pit entrance, a yard, and waiting while the carts come – horse and carts in those days – and as it fell off, it'd been overloaded, I picked it up and put it in the bucket. I took it home. That was before I went to school.

B: And there was no free ration of coal for miners?
R: None whatever.

B: No?
R: None whatever. None whatever.

B: How old would you be then, when you were doing this?
R: About ten or eleven.

B: Tell me about the school. What was that like?
R: Well, I went to a Catholic school . . . I was C of E but I went to a Catholic school because it was near at hand and they would allow C of E in them days. They didn't bother very much. And I attended a Catholic school and up to the time to starting working. And I had no option about pit life.

B: Did you have to pay to go to this school?
R: No. No.

B: What did you learn? I mean was it possible to learn much there?
R: No. No. They used to . . .

B: Why not?
R: Well, of course, they used to start off with religion first of all. You know. And then there was the ordinary way, geography and things like that. But not like it is today, I don't suppose. It was just the ordinary teaching.

B: And you first went to school at what age?
R: About six. Five or six. Something like that.

B: Did you learn, for instance, anything about the history of mining?
R: When I was young?

B: No. At school?
R: No.

B: Did you learn any kind of history? I mean did you learn about the Reform Bill?
R: Yes. The history that we learnt was about other countries. The capital of this country, the capital of that country. That's as far as we learned as far as history was concerned. As far as I can remember.

B: Yes. Then what age were you when you left school?
R: Fourteen.

B: And did you know then you had no choice but to go down the pit or did you hope to do something else?
R: I never had any option. The moment I was fourteen I had no option whatever. I had to go down the pit owing to financial circumstances. I was compelled to go down the pit to bring a little in to help to keep the home going. At fourteen years of age, and I got seven shillings and sixpence a week for working five days a week. I was down the pit ten hours a day which works out at two pennies per hour. At fourteen years of age.

B: Had your father talked about the pit? Did you know what to expect before you went down for the first time?
R: No. He didn't talk about the pit, but I'd seen men coming out . . . I'd heard them talking in different places and boys talking about it, and it seemed that everybody had one idea. To go to the pit. And nothing else was ever in their minds, of the fathers in them days. To put the boy to something which would benefit more as years went along.

B: And what was your first job in the pit?

R: The first job in the pit was at the pit bottom. Now, there's a pit tunnel as you get to the bottom of the pit, there's a tunnel, and that tunnel is where the coal comes from the workings. And there was horses because horses could pull fourteen to twenty tubs. There was tubs – seven-hundred-weight tubs. They used to bring them from the workings to the bottom of the pit, and our job was, as boys, to uncouple them with a view to men putting them in the cage to send them to the surface. And when the coal was going up to the surface the empty wagons in the cage were coming down and those empty wagons that came down were put round to us and we had to couple them up, and the horse was coupled up to those empty wagons and taken back into the workings which went to bring some full ones back. A kind of transport both ways.

B: The roads there . . .
R: Yes, the roads . . .

B: . . . would be quite large?
R: Oh, well, they wasn't too bad because there was horses, you see, and you had to keep them pretty high for their horses. There wasn't ponies that I've seen in other pits. It was horses.

B: What kind of lighting system did they have in these main roads?
R: Lights?

B: Yes.
R: Oh, there was lights. Only from about two hundred yards from the pit bottom there was lights. And there was no other light. The boy that used to look after the horse . . . and lead the horse, he had a lamp. A little oil lamp, that was. And the lights. You didn't see any more lights about two hundred yards when you left the pit bottom.

B: Now, after this first job, uncoupling the wagons . . .

R: Yes.

B: What was the next job you did?

R: Well, the next job . . . My father, it seems, was friendly with some fellers. Fellers worked together in threes. Three men worked together in a twenty-four-yard piece of coal. What they call the 'place', you see. And those three men worked there and they wanted a boy. So my father said that I could go with them. So I went to work with them at half a crown a day.

B: They paid you or the company paid you?

R: The men paid me. The firm didn't. The firm didn't employ me any more. I went and I worked with these three men. They paid me half a crown a day and for that half a crown I left the pit bottom. I had to go into the workings, and we went up three inclines that dipped one in three and four hundred yards.

B: One in three gradient?

R: One in three gradient and four hundred yards. Every one of them was, or more than that. And the last one was only about four feet high and men had to use sticks – the miners in those days had sticks to help them up these gradients to get to their place of work.

B: The gradients . . . was it because the roads were following the seam?

R: Yes, following the seam. Yes. The gradient following the seam. That's the correct term: 'following the seam'. And I tell you, I had half a crown a day for that and I worked with these men for a while.

B: What did the job consist of?

R: Well, you're what they call a 'drawer' or a 'waggoner'. Now a waggoner means – or a drawer means – you get the empty wagons and you take it to your men. They fill it with coal and you bring the full one away from them. And that's your job.

B: Pushing it?

R: Pushing it, and the roads were so low in those days that boys like me had to use a bow that clipped on top of the wagon because if the wagon tipped up you could cut your fingers off, and by having this bow when it tipped up your fingers were saved.

B: Were there accidents?

R: Oh yes. Yes. Plenty of accidents.

B: I mean with runaway wagons.

R: Oh yes. Yes, there were accidents at different times, you know. Different times, there was accidents. Such as rope breaking or . . .

B: Then what happened?

R: Well, if the rope broke, it might miss you and it might hit you. But there was . . .

B: Was there any room for you to get out of the way?

R: Not much, not much. Everything was cut narrow, you know, in them days. There wasn't much room.

B: Then how long did you go on doing this job as a boy?

R: Until I was sixteen.

B: Yes.

R: And then I could stay on. And when I stayed on then I'd go down the pit at quarter to six and I'd be down the pit till half past six. Half past six at night. And I might say that we've never seen daylight. Only at weekends. Week in, week out, month in, month out, and never saw daylight.

B: Twelve-hour shift?

R: Twelve hours – more than that many a time. And never saw daylight. And we was stripped – only clogs, socks and a pair of cotton drawers on. Stripped.

B: What was the temperature like?

R: Not too bad, not too bad.

B: And the ventilation?

R: Well, it was . . . not too bad. You couldn't call it warm but you'd sweat, you know. You'd sweat if you was very busy.

B: And the flow of air was reasonable?

R: Reasonable.

B: Adequate or not?

R: Oh, reasonable, oh yes. Yes, it was reasonable.

B: Then when did you become a collier? On the coal face?

R: When I was about nineteen. Then I worked with my uncle when I was about nineteen, and we worked nights. We used to go nights. Go down the pit. It was six o'clock and come up maybe half past five, five o'clock or half past on the morning after. And I've known us go down the pit – we've had a lamp each, oil lamp – I've known me get without light before I've been down two or three hours and I've done rest of the shift in total darkness. And guess what I was doing?

B: What?
R: Feeling for what I was doing. Touch. Touch. I've been down the pit . . .

B: But in the darkness did you sing?
R: You tried to be as cheerful as you could . . .

B: Otherwise you'd go mad.
R: Well. I . . . I've been hours at once feeling my way. Hours at once feeling my way because it got without a light, and if you had to get another light, you'd have to come to the pit bottom which was perhaps three quarters of a mile away and your living was going and there was no other way of getting a light. And I groped in the dark for hours on end.

B: This is actually at the coal face.
R: At the coal face.

B: How high would the working be?
R: Eh . . . well, it was a tall seam in them days. It was about six foot.

B: Yes.
R: Because I'd gone from the seams that were shallow – two foot or two foot six – and I was working in a six-foot seam then.

B: How much mechanisation was there, if any?
R: None.

B: None at all?
R: None at all.

B: What about when you undercut the seam?

R: You had to do it all with pick and spade. You had to slog it out. There was no mechanisation at all.

B: What about for scraping the coal away? Did you have to do this with a shovel?

R: No, no.

B: Not with a shovel? What did you do then?

R: You had a wagon close to you, or a tub . . .

B: Yes.

R: . . . and as you got the coal you put it in the tub. Mechanisation wasn't even in existence then at all. It simply had to be done with pure slogging.

B: What tools did you have?

R: Pick. And you had what they call the blade. That fitted on, you know, and you had a spade and a hammer and two or three blades and a shaft – a big shaft – and those were the tools you had.

B: And did you do the drilling yourself?

R: There was no drilling. We . . .

B: There wasn't any drilling?

R: No.

B: What about . . . not for the shot firing?

R: No. We had no shots.

B: None?

R: No.

B: So everything had to be taken down manually with a pick.
R: Yes. In them days. Yes.

B: How much coal could you shift in a night or day?
R: Well . . .

B: It depended?
R: It just depended on the nature of the place you was in. Sometimes it was very hard and sometimes it was better than others. It's just amazing that in mines like that, where you can go in a place and the coal is not too bad to get; in others, just like solid rock. I've known us go to work and only fill three tubs in a day.

B: How much would that earn you?
R: Well, that would be about two bob.

B: That's for three of you?
R: Well, that'd be three tubs each.

B: Yes. I see.
R: You see?

B: Yep.
R: Three tubs each. That would be two bob each.

B: And on a good day how many tubs could you fill if the conditions were good enough?
R: On a good day? Well, you might fill about six or seven.

B: Yes.
R: And in them days every tonne of coal that you filled you had to fill twenty-one hundredweight to the tonne, the management

took . . . or the firm . . . they took hundredweight out of every tonne – claimed you was throwing dirt in. You had to fill twenty-one hundredweight to the tonne. In them days.

B: When you were working like this on these twelve-hour shifts how much time could you take off to have something to eat or drink, or simply a blow – a rest?

R: Well, we used to eat our food about twice, but there was many a time if you was busy you'd eat it as you were going along.

B: Whilst you were working?

R: Yes. You'd have a bite and put it down and when you come out again you'd have another bite. But sometimes you'd be . . . in long hours like that, there was many a time we had long waits. Something was happening, and you'd have your food then. While the opportunity presented itself. So you could have your food and then when the tubs come you was ready for action.

B: What about drink? Did you drink a lot in that kind of temperature?

R: Oh yes. You'd drink three or four pints of water, but I've been in pits where I've wanted six or seven pints of water and drunk it.

B: What were the safety regulations like? For big accidents? For explosions? Or fallen coal?

R: Well . . . I . . . it's very difficult to say. With regard to the accidents, you see, there wasn't the same care taken then as there is now. And it was up to you as a miner to see and look after yourself to the best of your ability. They would supply you with timber for props and things like that to try and keep themselves safe and things like that. They would send you timber and all things like that, and bars and . . . weren't always there when you needed them.

B: Well, then you would go on cutting without propping.

R: There wasn't cutting. It was getting it with the pick.

B: Yep.

R: But, eh . . .

B: But you've gone picking without propping?

R: Yes. You was taking unnecessary risks in them days because the props weren't always there when you needed them you see. At times it was alright [but] they wasn't always there every time.

B: What was the sort of rate? Not of . . . I'm not now talking about serious accidents . . .

R: Yes, yes, yes . . .

B: . . . disasters. Simply of minor injuries.

R: Yes.

B: What was the rate of that? I mean . . . how often would a collier at that time get minorly hurt. Slightly hurt?

R: Well, he . . . I should say on an average he'd get about four bump a year.

B: And a bump might consist of what?

R: Well, being off several weeks.

B: From fallings.

R: Well. Might be coal come and hit him in the legs or something hit him on the head. We'd no helmets in them days, you know. No helmets on . . . you had no hat on. You were simply stripped with nothing on.

B: How did you carry the lamp if it wasn't on your helmet?

R: Well, I used to have a piece of string round me neck and it was – you was an artist really. You had to be. You had to kind of go with the swing. And keep your light in like that. And the slightest mistake and your light was out. And you used to have it round your neck and some chaps carried it and worked with it in the mouth. I've seen men with them in the mouth for hours on end. In the mouth.

B: Providing that you were fit, was work regular?
R: Yes. Five day a week for us then. Yes. Oh yes.

B: With not much unemployment?
R: No. No. There wasn't much unemployment then.

B: Now of this, your wage, thirty-five bob. How would this be spent when you took it home?
R: Well, me mother had tried to . . . it was a blessing to me mother to bring back, you know. And she would add that to what me dad got and, well . . . we carried on. It was a little bit better than what we did before I started to work.

B: How much did you keep for yourself?
R: I didn't keep anything. My mother used to give it me back – what I asked for.

B: And how much would she be able to give you back?
R: About five bob.

B: A week?
R: Yes.

B: How would you spend that five bob?
R: Well, there's not pictures then. Eh . . . Well, I used to buy

cigarettes, smoking on the sly and things like that, you know. And they used to come shows on the market in them days, you know. Acting. And it was fourpence to go in and you had . . .

B: What sort of shows?
R: Acting. Drama.

B: Yes.
R: And there was good acting in them days. I remember it all so well. Well, we used to go in there and think we were on top of the world. If we was going to a show like that.

B: Yes.
R: And then. And then after a while, you know, there was the Salford Hippodrome down there. We used to go down there. Well, it was only . . . you could go down there and you could go and watch the show and come out, have some cigarettes and buy yourself a box of matches for a shilling. And that was your night out.

B: What kind of way were miners treated at that time by other people who were not miners; – not in the pits?
R: Well, if I must give you my honest opinion, they just thought the scum of the earth, because in them days we had what they call a demonstration at Blackpool – a miners' demonstration – and that was as early as fifty-odd years ago. And the old tale goes that when the miners come, the people – the residents – were surprised. They thought they had tails. They thought the miners had tails. That was the general conversation. But after a while when they realised what an acquisition they was to the country they changed their minds about this tail.

B: What about other workers? I mean workers in industry. What kind of opinion did they have of miners?

R: Well, they might not have said it but I always thought that they didn't swallow a miner too well. They thought it was degrading to be down there.

B: Degrading?

R: Well, I had that feeling. At times. From some people I have met, from what they've said. Reading between the lines, you know.

B: Now when you get home having done your shift, what kind of facilities were there for washing? I mean certainly there was nothing at the pithead, or was there?

R: No. There was no facilities for washing at all. What we had to do – most men did it – you washed round here, round here under your arms and I used to get a rough towel . . .

B: This is in the kitchen sink, is it?

R: Yes. In the kitchen. And close the middle door. If you had a middle door. I used to rub me down with a rough towel – and rub all the rough off, and then sleep in something that was long to stop the bedding from getting dirty, because if you didn't, either your wife or your mother was everlasting washing. And I've known mothers with four sons had to wash pit drawers every night of the week that's been wet through with sweat, and they've had to wash them pit drawers before theirs lads could go to work the morning after else they was raw round here with sweating.

B: Did you ever get a bath?

R: No. Unless I went to the public baths.

B: How often could you do that?

R: I could go every week if I wanted, but it was . . . you

hadn't a lot of money, and coppers . . . was vital then, and you managed somehow, you know. And perhaps you'd go and get over some fields and dive in some water which I'd done many a time.

B: Did you go on holidays?

R: No. Not until I . . . I never had holiday until I was twenty. And I might say . . . I might tell you how I got holiday too. How I had money for a holiday was this: I saved up two shillings a week in what they call a factory club. The money was taken to the cotton mill, two shillings a week . . . and when you'd saved up twelve months you'd five gold sovereign. And the first five gold sovereigns that was, I thought I had . . . I thought I had more money than ever Churchill had! And that was twenty years of age before I had holiday.

B: And when you had a holiday it was unpaid. No pay?

R: No pay attached to it at all. In fact when we'd had a holiday – when we'd come back from the holidays – it was often as not your mother's got to go to the shop and get your food on tick until you could get a wage. And that's how we lived.

B: A few weeks ago in Derbyshire there was a new mine, or rather a reconditioned mine where at the coal face it is completely automatic . . .

R: Yes.

B: Where no men at all . . .

R: Yes.

B: The propping, cutting . . .

R: Yes, yes.

B: . . . is all done by machinery.

R: Yes. Mechanical.

B: The whole thing. No one at the coal face. What do you think about that now?

R: Well, it's the wonder of the age. It's a wonder of the age.

B: Now if this process went on, you would eventually have something where almost all of the work would be automated in the mines.

R: Yes.

B: And there would no longer be . . . miners in the sense that we now understand them.

R: Quite so.

B: What do you think about that?

R: Well, that is so. If that . . . if that goes on and is . . . but . . . I might tell you this: that it's easier to do that in a flat seam – this is a gradient seam.

B: But if this happened, would you welcome it?

R: Yes.

B: I mean you would like to see the time . . .

R: Yes.

B: . . . when there aren't any miners?

R: I would. From what I've experienced . . . from what I've experienced I wouldn't like a dog of mine to go in. From what I've experienced. In the pits. And if my lad would have lived, I can tell you this: he'd never have gone in the mine.

The Nature of Mass Demonstrations
New Society, *23 May 1968*

Seventy years ago (on 6 May 1898) there was a massive demonstration of workers, men and women, in the centre of Milan. The events which led up to it involve too long a history to treat with here. The demonstration was attacked and broken up by the army under the command of General Beccaris. At noon the cavalry charged the crowd, the unarmed workers tried to make barricades, martial law was declared, and for three days the army fought against the unarmed.

The official casualty figures were 100 workers killed and 450 wounded. One policeman was killed accidentally by a soldier. There were no army casualties. (Two years later Umberto I was assassinated because after the massacre he publicly congratulated General Beccaris, the 'butcher of Milan'.)

I have been trying to understand certain aspects of the demonstration in the Corso Venezia on 6 May because of a story I am writing. In the process I came to a few conclusions about demonstrations which may perhaps be more widely applicable.

Mass demonstrations should be distinguished from riots or revolutionary uprisings although, under certain (now rare) circumstances, they may develop into either of the latter. The aims of a riot are usually immediate (the immediacy matching the desperation they express): the seizing of food, the release of prisoners, the destruction of property. The aims of a revolutionary uprising are long-term and comprehensive: they culminate in the taking over of State power. The aims of a demonstration, however, are symbolic: it demonstrates a force that is scarcely used.

A large number of people assemble together in an obvious and already announced public place. They are more or less unarmed. (On 6 May 1898, entirely unarmed.) They present themselves as a target to the forces of repression serving the State authority against whose policies they are protesting.

Theoretically demonstrations are meant to reveal the strength of popular opinion or feeling: theoretically they are an appeal to the democratic conscience of the State. But this presupposes a conscience which is very unlikely to exist.

If the State authority is open to democratic influence, the demonstration will hardly be necessary; if it is not, it is unlikely to be influenced by an empty show of force containing no real threat. (A demonstration in support of an already established alternative State authority – as when Garibaldi entered Naples in 1860 – is a special case and may be immediately effective.)

Demonstrations took place before the principle of democracy was even nominally admitted. The massive early Chartist demonstrations were part of the struggle to obtain such an admission. The crowds who gathered to present their petition to the Tsar in St Petersburg in 1905 were appealing – and presenting themselves as a target – to the ruthless power of an absolute monarchy. In the event – as on so many hundreds of other occasions all over Europe – they were shot down.

It would seem that the true function of demonstrations is not to convince the existing State authority to any significant degree. Such an aim is only a convenient rationalisation.

The truth is that mass demonstrations are rehearsals for revolution: not strategic or even tactical ones, but rehearsals of revolutionary awareness. The delay between the rehearsals and the real performance may be very long: their quality – the intensity of rehearsed awareness – may, on different occasions, vary considerably: but any demonstration which lacks this element of rehearsal is better described as an officially encouraged public spectacle.

A demonstration, however much spontaneity it may contain, is a created event which arbitrarily separates itself from ordinary life. Its value is the result of its artificiality, for therein lies its prophetic, rehearsing possibilities.

A mass demonstration distinguishes itself from other mass crowds because it congregates in public to create its function, instead of forming in response to one: in this, it differs from any assembly of workers within their place of work – even when strike action is involved – or from any crowd of spectators. It is an assembly which challenges what is given by the mere fact of its coming together.

State authorities usually lie about the number of demonstrators involved. The lie, however, makes little difference. (It would only make a significant difference if demonstrations really were an appeal to the democratic conscience of the State.) The importance of the numbers involved is to be found in the direct experience of those taking part in or sympathetically witnessing the demonstration. For them the numbers cease to be numbers and become the evidence of their senses, the conclusions of their imagination. The larger the demonstration, the more powerful and immediate (visible, audible, tangible) a metaphor it becomes for their total collective strength.

I say metaphor because the strength thus grasped transcends the potential strength of those present, and certainly their actual strength as deployed in a demonstration. The more people there are there, the more forcibly they represent to each other and to themselves those who are absent. In this way a mass demonstration simultaneously extends and gives body to an abstraction. Those who take part become more positively aware of how they belong to a class. Belonging to that class ceases to imply a common fate and implies a common opportunity. They begin to recognise that the function of their class need no longer be limited: that it, too, like the demonstrations itself, can create its own function.

Revolutionary awareness is rehearsed in another way by the choice and effect of location. Demonstrations are essentially urban in character, and they are usually planned to take place as near as possible to some symbolic centre, either civic or national. Their 'targets' are seldom the strategic ones – railway stations, barracks, radio stations, airports. A mass demonstration can be interpreted as the symbolic capturing of a city or capital. Again, the symbolism or metaphor is for the benefit of the participants.

The demonstration, an irregular event created by the demonstrators, nevertheless takes place near the city centre, intended for very different uses. The demonstrators interrupt the regular life of the streets they march through or of the open spaces they fill. They 'cut off' these areas, and, not yet having the power to occupy them permanently, they transform them into a temporary stage on which they dramatise the power they still lack.

The demonstrators' view of the city surrounding their stage also changes. By demonstrating, they manifest a greater freedom and independence – a greater creativity, even although the product is only symbolic – than they can ever achieve individually or collectively when pursuing their regular lives. In their regular pursuits they only modify circumstances; by demonstrating they symbolically oppose their very existence to circumstances.

This creativity may be desperate in origin, and the price to be paid for it high, but it temporarily changes their outlook. They become corporately aware that it is they or those whom they represent who have built the city and who maintain it. They see it through different eyes. They see it as their product, confirming their potential instead of reducing it.

Finally, there is another way in which revolutionary awareness is rehearsed. The demonstrators present themselves as a target to the so-called forces of law and order. Yet the larger the target they present, the stronger they feel. This cannot be explained by the banal principle of 'strength in numbers', any more than by vulgar theories of crowd psychology. The contradiction between their actual vulnerability and their sense of invincibility corresponds to the dilemma which they force upon the State authority.

Either authority must abdicate and allow the crowd to do as it wishes: in which case the symbolic suddenly becomes real, and, even if the crowd's lack of organisation and preparedness prevents it from consolidating its victory, the event demonstrates the weakness of authority. Or else authority must constrain and disperse the crowd with violence: in which case the undemocratic character of such authority is publicly displayed. The imposed dilemma is between displayed weakness and displayed authoritarianism. (The officially approved and controlled demonstration does not impose the same dilemma: its symbolism is censored, which is why I term it a mere public spectacle.) Almost invariably, authority chooses to use force. The extent of its violence depends upon many factors, but scarcely ever upon the scale of the physical threat offered by the demonstrators. This threat is essentially symbolic. But by attacking the demonstration authority ensures that the symbolic event becomes an historical one: an event to be remembered, to be learnt from, to be avenged.

It is in the nature of a demonstration to provoke violence upon itself. Its provocation may also be violent. But in the end it is bound to suffer more than it inflicts. This is a tactical truth and an historical one. The historical role of demonstrations is to show the injustice, cruelty, irrationality of the existing State authority. Demonstrations are protests of innocence.

But the innocence is of two kinds, which can only be treated as though they were one at a symbolic level. For the purposes of political analysis and the planning of revolutionary action, they must be separated. There is an innocence to be defended and an innocence which must finally be lost: an innocence which derives from justice and an innocence which is the consequence of a lack of experience.

Demonstrations express political ambitions before the political means necessary to realise them have been created. Demonstrations predict the realisation of their own ambitions and thus may contribute to that realisation, but they cannot themselves achieve them.

The question which revolutionaries must decide in any given historical situation is whether or not further symbolic rehearsals are necessary. The next stage is training in tactics and strategy for the performance itself.

Acknowledgements

The editors would like to thank the Berger Estate, Guy Lavender, Espen Bale, Ian Greaves, Simon Thorogood, Leila Cruickshank, Luke Ingram and Gareth Evans for their help assembling this collection. Special thanks to Scott King and Tom Etherington for designing Berger's *Germinal* essay.

'Peerless'
SUSAN SONTAG

CANON**GATE